Dog Heroes®

Shelter Dogs

by Meish Goldish

Consultant: Faith Maloney, Cofounder and Animal Care Consultant
Best Friends Animal Society
Kanab, Utah

Bearport Publishing

New York, New York

Credits

Cover and Title Page, © Roman Samokhin/Shutterstock; Cover TR, © Getty Images; Cover CR, Courtesy of National Disaster Search Dog Foundation; Cover BR, Courtesy of Dawn Tibbetts; TOC, © Sharon Hanzelka; 4, Courtesy of the Parker County Sheriff's Office/Deputy Danie Huffman; 5, © spcaLA; 6, © Jupiter Images; 7, © Associated Press; 8, © John Moore/Getty Images; 9, © Getty Images; 10, © MCT via Getty Images; 11, © Lara Cerri/ZUMA Press/Corbis; 12–13, Courtesy of Dawn Tibbetts; 13, © Brian Snyder/Reuters/Corbis; 14 © L.A. Nature Graphics; 15, Courtesy of Dawn Tibbetts; 16, © Arterra Picture Library/Alamy; 17, © Denver Post via Getty Images; 18, Courtesy of National Disaster Search Dog Foundation; 19, © Denise Sanders; 20, © Sharon Hanzelka; 21, © Associated Press; 22, © John Sipple, Courtesy of Topanga Messenger; 23, © J. J. Guillen/EPANewscom; 24, © The Washington Post/Getty Images; 25, © Todd Heisler/The New York Times; 26, © Roman Samokhin/Shutterstock; 27, © Augusta DeLisi, Augie's Doggies Rescue; 28, © iStockphoto/Thinkstock; 29TL, © Gualtiero Boffi/Shutterstock; 29TR, © Eric Isselee/Shutterstock; 29BL, © iStockphoto/Thinkstock; 29BR, © Eric Isselee/Shutterstock.

Publisher: Kenn Goin
Senior Editor: Joyce Tavolacci
Creative Director: Spencer Brinker
Design: Dawn Beard Creative
Photo Researcher: Picture Perfect Professionals, LLC

Library of Congress Cataloging-in-Publication Data

Goldish, Meish.
Shelter dogs / by Meish Goldish.
pages cm. — (Dog heroes)
Includes bibliographical references and index.
ISBN-13: 978-1-61772-886-0 (library binding)
ISBN-10: 1-61772-886-1 (library binding)
1. Dogs—Juvenile literature. 2. Animal shelters—Juvenile literature. 3. Dog adoption—Juvenile literature. I. Title.
SF426.5.G646 2014
636.7'0832—dc23
2013003085

For more information, write to Bearport Publishing Company, Inc., 45 West 21st Street, Suite 3B, New York, New York 10010. Printed in the United States of America.

10 9 8 7 6 5 4 3 2 1

Table of Contents

A Dog Named Bear 4

Racing Against Time 6

Animal Shelters 8

Caring for Shelter Dogs 10

A Rocky Start 12

Rocky to the Rescue 14

Prison Pets 16

Teaching to Search 18

The Life of Riley 20

Buried Alive 22

War Wounds 24

A Lifesaver 26

Just the Facts 28

Common Breeds: Shelter Dogs 29

Glossary 30

Bibliography 31

Read More 31

Learn More Online 31

Index 32

About the Author 32

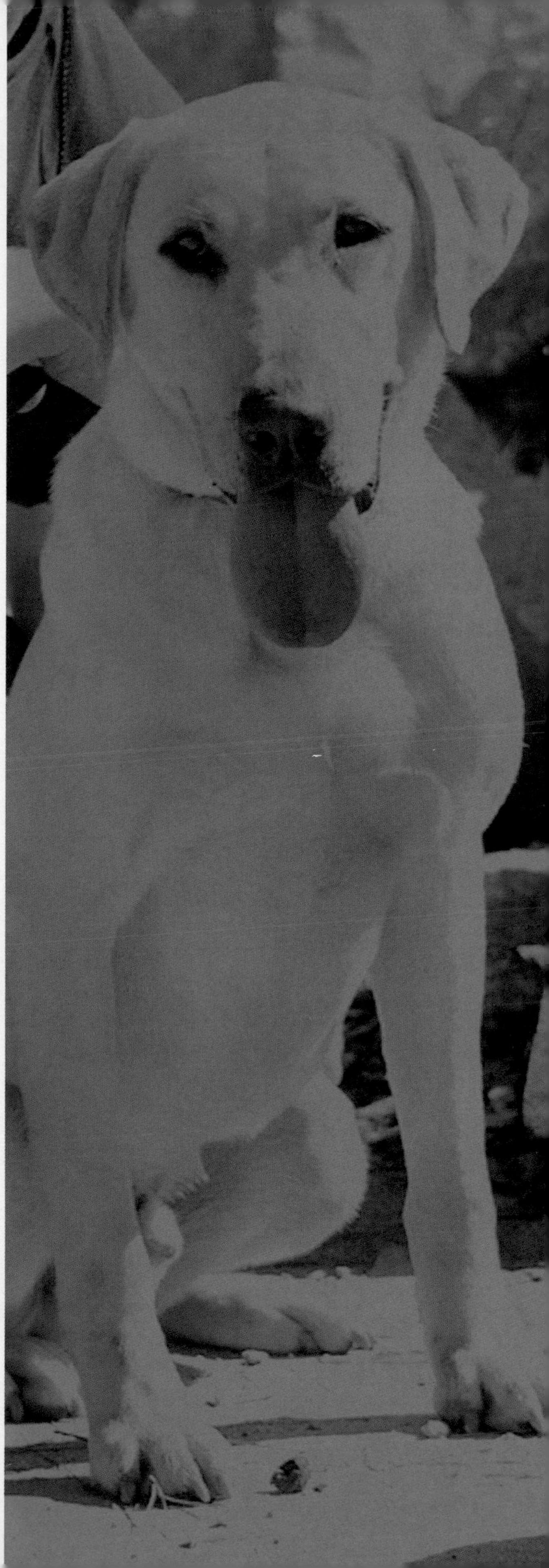

A Dog Named Bear

In 2010, Debbie Zeisler **adopted** a huge dog named Bear from an **animal shelter** in Texas. Debbie, who suffers from **seizures**, felt an immediate connection with the 100-pound (45 kg) German shepherd. Little did Debbie know that one day Bear would save her life.

Debbie Zeisler with her dog, Bear

Experts believe that Bear can smell a special scent that Debbie's body gives off before she has a seizure.

One hot summer day in 2011, Debbie left her house to check her mailbox. All of a sudden, Bear blocked her path by moving his body in front of hers. He sensed that she was going to have a seizure. Unaware of what was coming and eager to get her mail, Debbie continued walking. Then the seizure struck. Debbie fell down and banged her head. She lay **unconscious** in front of her house. Could Bear help her?

Some dogs can be trained to know when their owner is about to have a seizure. However, Bear never received any training.

Racing Against Time

As Debbie lay on the ground, Bear ran to get help. Using his large paws, Bear scratched on the front door of each neighbor's home. Luckily, two **animal control officers** finally spotted the dog. As soon as they saw the tag on Bear's collar that identified him as a **service dog**, they knew they had to find his owner. The officers quickly searched the neighborhood until they found Debbie's house.

When Bear and the officers arrived, Debbie was awake but dizzy and confused. The officers called an ambulance. Luckily, Debbie recovered quickly from her fall. For his quick action, Bear received the National Hero Dog Award from the SPCA of Los Angeles in 2012. "This just goes to show how amazing shelter dogs can be," said the SPCA's president.

SPCA stands for the Society for the Prevention of Cruelty to Animals. The organization works to keep animals healthy and safe from abuse.

"I rescued him. He rescued me," said Debbie, speaking of her special companion, Bear.

Animal Shelters

Like Bear, many dogs are adopted from animal shelters. These are organizations that care for homeless pets and try to find homes for them. While shelters take in many kinds of animals, most of the pets who live there are dogs and cats. Each year, as many as three million dogs are placed in shelters in the United States.

Animal shelters such as this one care for hundreds of animals.

Why are so many dogs put into shelters? Sometimes, their owners become ill or don't have time to care for them. As a result, owners might drop off their pets at a shelter, hoping someone will adopt them. Other times, people simply **abandon** their pets on the streets. Abandoned dogs become **strays** that are forced to live on their own. Luckily, animal control officers are often able to catch these **canines** and bring them to a shelter to be cared for.

An animal control officer bringing a stray dog to a shelter

There are between 3,500 and 5,000 animal shelters in the United States.

Caring for Shelter Dogs

Once a dog arrives at a shelter, workers care for it and prepare it for adoption. They do many of the same jobs that dog owners would do. For example, they make sure the dog is healthy and receives medical care. They feed the canine and give it clean water to drink. They keep its living area clean too.

A shelter worker cares for two Chihuahuas.

Many shelters are crowded with hundreds of dogs. Workers try their best to get each dog adopted. Sadly, not all of the dogs find homes. At some animal shelters, dogs that aren't adopted are put to sleep.

This homeless dog was just taken for a walk by a shelter worker.

More than half of all shelter dogs in the United States are put to sleep.

A Rocky Start

Rocky was a stray that roamed near the Lassen County Animal Shelter in California. For days, shelter workers tried to catch the yellow dog. However, the frightened canine wouldn't let anyone near him. When Rocky was finally caught, shelter workers saw that he was injured, hungry, and very shy.

Rocky (above) was afraid of people, probably because he didn't have much contact with them when he was a pup.

Because Rocky was so afraid of people, workers worried that he would never get adopted. As a result, they decided to place him in a program called Pups on Parole. In this program, prisoners prepare homeless dogs for adoption. Rocky was paired with a prisoner who showered him with love and attention. Over time, the once fearful dog became friendly and relaxed around people.

By showing the dogs in their care love, prisoners receive a lot of love in return.

In the Pups on Parole program, prisoners **house-train** their dogs and teach them basic **commands** such as *come, sit,* and *stay*. Most importantly, they give the dogs lots of love.

Rocky to the Rescue

After Rocky finished his training, a prison worker named Dawn Tibbets adopted him. "I looked at him and he looked at me . . . and I just couldn't leave him," said Dawn. After bringing him home, Rocky immediately **bonded** with Dawn's husband, Floyd. One day, Floyd took Rocky on a hike in a far-off **canyon**. While walking in the canyon, Floyd collapsed with chest pains. Rocky stayed by Floyd's side and licked his hand until he was alert again.

A canyon in northern California like the one that Floyd went hiking in

After Floyd was feeling a little stronger, he tried to walk back to his car—but he walked in the wrong direction. Luckily, his loving dog guided him all the way to the car. Rocky was a hero. The yellow canine that had been rescued from the street had now saved his owner's life!

Rocky and his owner, Floyd

Since 2007, more than 300 dogs, including Rocky, have been adopted after being trained by prisoners in the Pups on Parole program.

Prison Pets

Prison Pet Partnership (PPP) is another program that helps homeless pups. Located in Washington State, it rescues canines from shelters and trains them to be service dogs. Service dogs help people who have medical problems do everyday things, such as turn on the lights or safely cross the street.

A woman in a wheelchair with her service dog

Like Pups on Parole, PPP pairs shelter dogs with prisoners who care for the animals. Prisoners learn how to feed, **groom**, and train their canines. The training period for each dog lasts about eight months. Then the dog is matched with a person who can use the canine's help.

A prisoner caring for a dog in the PPP program

Since Prison Pet Partnership began in 1982, over 700 trained dogs have gone on to help people in need.

Teaching to Search

Some shelter dogs become skilled rescuers. Wilma Melville runs the Search Dog Foundation (SDF) in Ojai, California. She takes in shelter dogs and trains them to be **search-and-rescue dogs**. These dogs are taught to search for **survivors** after **disasters** such as earthquakes, floods, and **terrorist** attacks. Once trained, each canine is paired with a **handler**. Working as a team, the handler and the dog search for survivors.

Wilma Melville with two of her furry companions

Wilma started her organization in 1996, not long after terrorists blew up a building in Oklahoma City. Wilma and her dog, a black Labrador named Murphy, traveled to Oklahoma City to look for survivors. After the experience, Wilma realized there was a great need for more search-and-rescue teams to help people affected by disasters.

SDF search-and-rescue teams

Dogs make excellent search animals because of their powerful sense of smell. They can smell a human as far away as half a mile (0.8 km).

The Life of Riley

Another shelter dog that has been trained to help out in disasters is a yellow Labrador named Riley. Because Riley was extremely **energetic**, no one wanted to adopt him. However, Wilma knew that with the right training, Riley would make a great search dog—and she was right.

Riley with his handler, Eric Gray

After Riley was rescued, the canine was taught how to climb a ladder and search for people trapped beneath rubble. His training "gave him a purpose," said Riley's handler, Eric Gray. In 2011, Riley and Eric joined six other Search Dog Foundation teams in northern Japan. They searched for survivors after a massive earthquake and **tsunami** destroyed the area.

Eric and Riley search for survivors after an earthquake and tsunami hit Japan in 2011.

The powerful earthquake and tsunami that struck Japan in 2011 damaged about one million buildings and killed close to 16,000 people.

Buried Alive

Another shelter dog that went on to save people's lives is Pearl. Like Riley, Pearl was rescued from an animal shelter by the SDF. After being trained, Pearl was paired with Ron Horetski, a Los Angeles firefighter.

Pearl with her handler, Fire Captain Ron Horetski

In 2010, Pearl and Ron joined other search teams to look for survivors after a huge earthquake struck Haiti, killing 300,000 people and destroying thousands of buildings. The dog sniffed for humans trapped as deep as 40 feet (12 m) underground. Pearl and the other canines located a dozen buried survivors, who were later rescued.

A rescue worker and his canine partner look for survivors under a building that fell during the 2010 earthquake in Haiti.

For her excellent search-and-rescue work, Pearl received the American Society for the Prevention of Cruelty to Animals (ASPCA) Dog of the Year Award in 2010.

War Wounds

Some shelter dogs are trained to help war **veterans.** Operation Heroes and Hounds (OHH) is a program that matches shelter dogs with veterans suffering from brain injuries or other problems after returning from war.

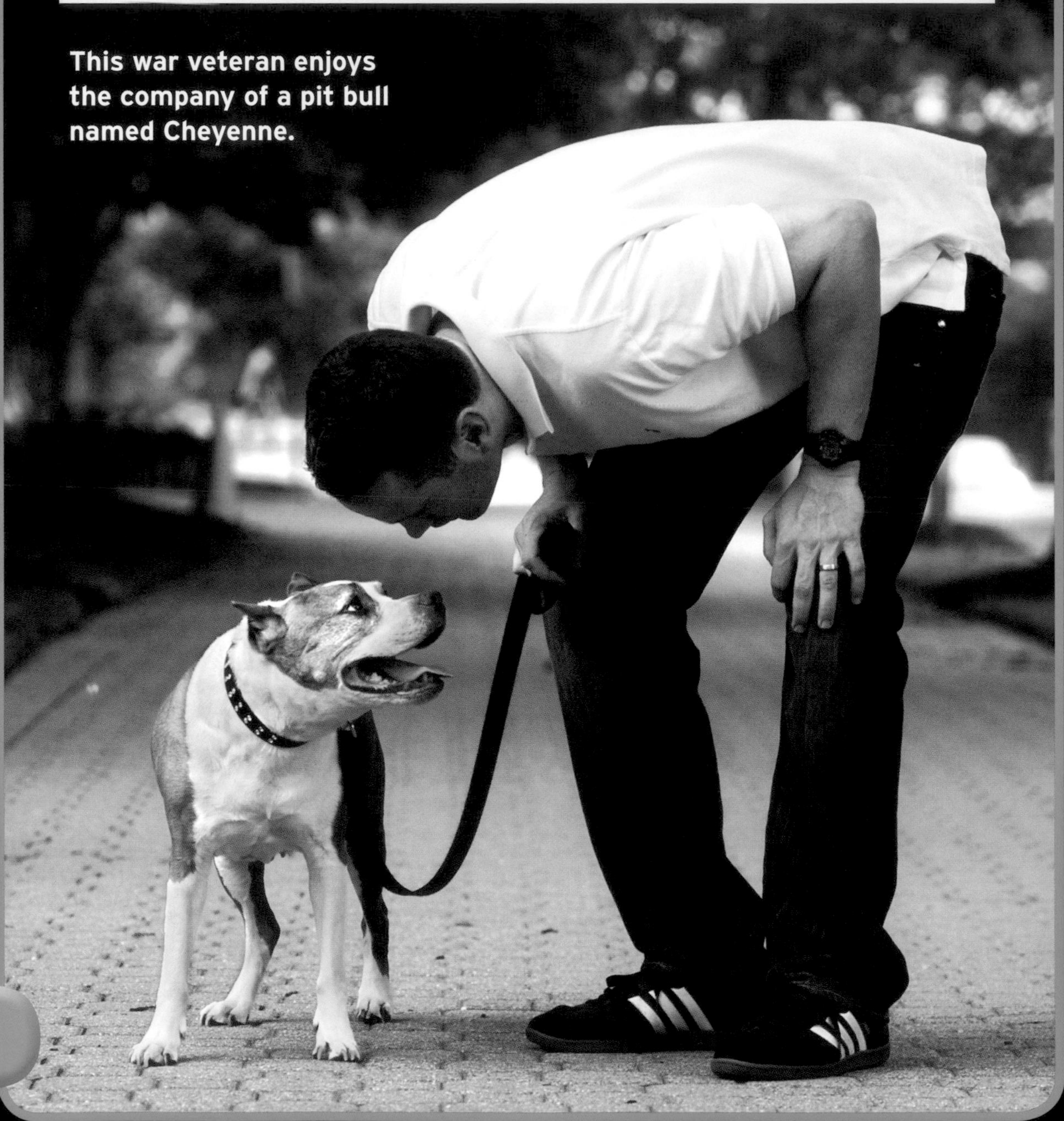

This war veteran enjoys the company of a pit bull named Cheyenne.

In the program, the vets learn how to train and care for their new pets. The canines, on the other hand, are taught how to behave and follow commands. Most important of all, each vet and dog gains a loving companion and learns to feel calm and safe. "We're all just one dog, one hug away from a better world," said one grateful veteran in the program.

Caring for and forming a bond with an animal can help a person, like this former soldier, gain confidence and feel more relaxed.

Some vets suffer from post-traumatic stress disorder (PTSD). PTSD is an illness that causes a person to feel very sad, nervous, and afraid.

A Lifesaver

Some young people are making sure that shelter dogs are given a chance to lead a good life. When Augusta DeLisi was 12 years old, she heard about a crowded animal shelter. The shelter planned to put many of its dogs to sleep if they weren't adopted within a week. With her family's help, Augusta rescued six dogs and quickly found a home for each one.

Augusta wanted to save even more shelter dogs, so she started Augies Doggies Rescue. Since 2002, Augies Doggies has rescued more than 125 homeless dogs and found loving homes for each of them. With caring friends like Augusta, dogs that were once unwanted are changing lives—one wet kiss at a time.

To ready the dogs for adoption, Augusta makes sure they get checked by a vet and are healthy.

Augusta DeLisi with a dog she rescued from a shelter

Just the Facts

- Some animal shelters put unwanted dogs to sleep if the shelter gets too crowded. However, others are "no-kill" shelters. They keep all of the animals in their care alive until they are adopted.
- Most of the workers at no-kill animal shelters are **volunteers**. Why? It's costly to pay workers, and many shelters cannot afford to do so. The volunteers are usually animal lovers who want to help homeless animals in any way they can.
- Animal shelters learn as much as they can about the dogs they take in, including how they behave. That way, workers can better match each animal with a person or family who wishes to adopt.

Common Breeds: SHELTER DOGS

Any kind of dog, including mixed breeds, can be placed in a shelter.

German shepherd

Labrador retriever

Pit bull

Mixed breed

abandon (uh-BAN-duhn) to leave alone and uncared for

abuse (uh-BYOOSS) cruel treatment

adopted (uh-DOPT-id) took into one's family

animal control officers (AN-uh-muhl kuhn-TROHL OF-uh-surz) people who catch stray animals

animal shelter (AN-uh-muhl SHEL-tur) a place that houses homeless or lost animals

bonded (BOND-id) to have a close friendship

canines (KAY-nyenz) members of the dog family

canyon (KAN-yuhn) a deep, narrow valley carved out by a river

commands (kuh-MANDZ) orders to do certain things

disasters (duh-ZASS-turz) events that cause great damage or loss

energetic (en-ur-JET-ik) active

groom (GROOM) to brush and clean

handler (HAND-lur) a person who trains and works with an animal that performs a job

house-train (HAUS-trayn) to teach an animal to go to the bathroom outside

search-and-rescue dogs (SURCH-AND-RES-kyoo DAWGZ) dogs that look for lost people after a disaster

seizures (SEE-zhurz) sudden attacks that can cause a person to shake and even lose consciousness

service dog (SUR-viss DAWG) a dog that is trained to help people who have health problems

strays (STRAYZ) animals that are lost or don't have homes

survivors (sur-VYE-vurz) people who live through a disaster or horrible event

terrorist (TER-ur-ist) having to do with people who use violence and terror to get what they want

tsunami (tsoo-NAH-mee) a huge wave or waves caused by an earthquake

unconscious (uhn-KON-shuhss) not awake

veterans (VET-ur-uhnz) people who have served in the armed forces

volunteers (*vol*-uhn-TIHRZ) people who work without pay

Bibliography

Kehret, Peg. *Shelter Dogs: Amazing Stories of Adopted Strays.* Morton Grove, IL: Albert Whitman (1999).

Leigh, Diane, and Marilee Geyer. *One at a Time: A Week in an American Animal Shelter.* Santa Cruz, CA: No Voice Unheard (2003).

Somerville, Bob. *Dogtown: A Sanctuary for Rescued Dogs.* South Portland, ME: Sellers (2008).

Read More

Fetty, Margaret. *Seizure-Alert Dogs (Dog Heroes).* New York: Bearport (2010).

Goldish, Meish. *Prison Puppies (Dog Heroes).* New York: Bearport (2011).

McDaniel, Melissa. *Disaster Search Dogs (Dog Heroes).* New York: Bearport (2005).

Tagliaferro, Linda. *Service Dogs (Dog Heroes).* New York: Bearport (2005).

Learn More Online

Visit these Web sites to learn more about shelter dogs:

www.augiesdoggiesrescue.org

www.bestfriends.org

www.paws.org/kids-volunteer.html

www.searchdogfoundation.org

Index

animal control officers 6–7, 8–9
animal shelters 8–9, 10–11, 28
ASPCA 23
Augies Doggies Rescue 26–27

Bear 4–5, 6–7, 8
brain injuries 24

cats 8
crowded shelters 11, 26–27, 28

DeLisi, Augusta 26–27

Gray, Eric 20–21

Horetski, Ron 22–23

Lassen County Animal Shelter 12–13

Melville, Wilma 18–19, 21
Murphy 19

"no-kill" shelters 28

Operation Heroes and Hounds 24–25

Pearl 22–23
Prison Pet Partnership 16–17
PTSD 25
Pups on Parole 12–13, 14–15, 17

Riley 20–21
Rocky 12–13, 14–15

search-and-rescue dogs 18–19, 20–21, 22–23
Search Dog Foundation (SDF) 18–19, 21
service dogs 6, 16–17
shelter volunteers 28
SPCA of Los Angeles 7
stray dogs 8–9, 12–13

Tibbets, Dawn and Floyd 14–15
training 12–13, 14–15, 16–17, 18–19, 20–21, 22–23, 24–25

war veterans 24–25

Zeisler, Debbie 4–5, 6–7

About the Author

Meish Goldish has written more than 200 books for children. His book *Dolphins in the Navy* received a Eureka! Honor Book Award from the California Reading Association in 2012.